The Greatest Gymnast of All

I swing. I jump. And then I shout,
"This is what I'm all about!"
I'm ZIPPING, ZOOMING ZOE—
the greatest gymnast of all.

I cartwheel on,

then off the mat.

My leaps are short,
or long—like that.

On and off, short and long,
I do it all 'cause I'm so strong.
I'm ZIPPING, ZOOMING ZOE—
the greatest gymnast of all.

Inside the hoop

and outside then.

I'm over the hoop,

and under again.

Inside, outside, over and under.
I think that I am truly a wonder.
I'm ZIPPING, ZOOMING ZOE—
the greatest gymnast of all.

A forward roll,

A backward flip.

I'm high—
then low.

I rarely slip.

Forward, backward, high and low.
I'm putting on a wonderful show.
I'm ZIPPING, ZOOMING ZOE—
the greatest gymnast of all.

I swing way up,

and down below.

My feet are near.

Out far they go.

Up and down, near and far.
I feel like I'm a superstar.

I'm ZIPPING, ZOOMING ZOE—
the greatest gymnast of all.

ACTIVITIES AT SCHOOL

The following activities will help you to extend children's understanding of the concepts presented in *The Greatest Gymnast of All:*

- Read the story with the children and ask them to describe what is happening in each picture.

- Throughout the story, ask questions about Zoe's positions, such as, 'Where is Zoe?', 'Where is she now?' and 'Is she over or under the hoop?' Use similar language to describe the actions of the children in their own P.E. lessons.

- Introduce the concept of opposites. For example, say, 'Near and far are opposites. What is the opposite of big?' Invite the class to think of some opposites of their own. Offer words such as 'hot', 'light' and 'old' for the children to find opposites to.

ACTIVITIES AT HOME

If you would like to have fun with the maths concepts presented in *The Greatest Gymnast of All*, here are a few suggestions:

- After reading the story with your child, ask him or her to retell it in his or her own words.

- Look at things outside the home and identify the opposites. Ask questions, for example, 'Is the little boy at the top of the slide or the bottom?', 'Which trees are near the house and which are far away?', 'Are there many cars parked along the street or just a few?', 'What moves slowly and what moves quickly?'

- Discuss all the opposites that can be found while taking a bath. Ask questions such as, 'When is the bath full and when is it empty?', 'Is the water hot or cold?' Practise turning the tap on and off. Describe hair, toys and flannels or sponges that are dry or wet, long or short, big or small.

- Ask each member of the family to pick a set of opposites and act them out. Encourage the rest of the family to guess what the opposites are.